Astronomers at Work

LAURA LORIA

Britannica®
Educational Publishing

IN ASSOCIATION WITH

ROSEN
EDUCATIONAL SERVICES

Published in 2018 by Britannica Educational Publishing (a trademark of Encyclopædia Britannica, Inc.) in association with The Rosen Publishing Group, Inc.
29 East 21st Street, New York, NY 10010

Distributed exclusively by Rosen Publishing.
To see additional Britannica Educational Publishing titles, go to rosenpublishing.com.

First Edition

Britannica Educational Publishing
J.E. Luebering: Executive Director, Core Editorial
Mary Rose McCudden: Editor, Britannica Student Encyclopedia

Rosen Publishing
Amelie von Zumbusch: Editor
Nelson Sá: Art Director
Nicole Russo-Duca: Designer
Cindy Reiman: Photography Manager
Karen Huang: Photo Researcher

Library of Congress Cataloging-in-Publication Data

Names: Loria, Laura, author.
Title: Astronomers at work / Laura Loria.
Description: First edition. | New York : Britannica Educational Publishing in
Association with Rosen Educational Services, 2018. | Series: Scientists at
work | Includes bibliographical references and index.
Identifiers: LCCN 2016056500 | ISBN 9781680487473 (library bound book : alk. paper) | ISBN 9781680487459
(pbk. book : alk. paper) | ISBN 9781680487466 (6 pack : alk. paper)
Subjects: LCSH: Astronomy—Vocational guidance—Juvenile literature. |
Astronomers—Juvenile literature. | Astronomy—Juvenile literature.
Classification: LCC QB51.5 .L67 2018 | DDC 520.023—dc23
LC record available at https://lccn.loc.gov/2016056500

Manufactured in the United States of America

Photo credits: Cover, p. 1 © iStockphoto.com/ClaudioVentrella; p. 4 ESA/NASA/Hubble; p. 5 Lester Lefkowitz/Iconica/Getty Images; pp. 6, 21 Encyclopædia Britannica, Inc.; p. 7 Jet Propulsion Laboratory/NASA; p. 8 CFHT/NOAO/AURA/NSF/NASA/ESA/STScI; p. 9 Rick Whitacre/Shutterstock.com; p. 10 Dan Kitwood/Getty Images; p. 11 Ariel Skelley/Blend Images/Getty Images; p. 12 Tylerfinvold; p. 13 NASA/Dryden/Tom Tschida; p. 14 Michael Stravato/The New York Times/Redux; p. 15 Two Micron All Sky Survey (2MASS), a joint project of the University of Massachusetts and the Infrared Processing and Analysis Center/California Institute of Technology, funded by NASA and the National Science Foundation; p. 16 Chief Warrant Officer 4 Seth Rossman/US Navy photo; p. 17 NASA; p. 18 Jonathan Larsen/Fotolia; p. 19 Hubble SM4 ERO Team & M-ESA/NASA; p. 20 ESO; p. 22 Adam Hart-Davis/Science Source; p. 23 ESO/M.-R. Cioni/VISTA Magellanic Cloud survey/Cambridge Astronomical Survey Unit; p. 24 © Photos.com/Thinkstock; p. 25 Leemage/Universal Images Group/Getty Images; p. 26 Babak Tafreshi/Science Source/Getty Images; p. 27 Vector FX/Shutterstock.com; p. 28 NASA, ESA, and the Hubble Heritage Team (STScI/AURA); p. 29 NASA/JPL-Caltech; interior pages background Teemu Tretjakov/Shutterstock.com.

Contents

An Ancient Science

Astronomy is one of the oldest sciences in the world. Thousands of years ago there were no calendars or clocks. People kept track of time by watching the sun and the stars. It was important for them to know the time in order to plant their crops and gather their harvests. These people were the first astronomers.

The study of astronomy involves all of the objects outside Earth's atmosphere. These include the sun, moon,

An astronomer's job involves identifying objects in space, such as the stars and clouds of gas and dust in this image.

4

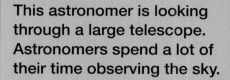

This astronomer is looking through a large telescope. Astronomers spend a lot of their time observing the sky.

planets, stars, galaxies, and all other **matter** in the universe. An astronomer's job is to observe, measure, and interpret the data they collect about these objects. This knowledge helps us understand what happens in space and how it affects us here on Earth.

What's Up There?

The closest star to planet Earth is our sun. It is the center of the solar system. The solar system consists of the sun and everything that orbits, or travels around, the sun. This includes the eight planets and their moons, dwarf planets, and countless asteroids, comets, and other small, icy objects. However, even with all these things, most of the solar system is empty space.

The solar system itself is only a small part of a huge system of stars and other

This diagram compares the sizes of the planets in the solar system. It shows them closer together than they actually are.

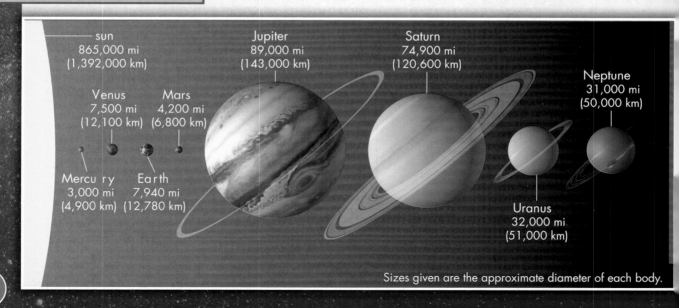

sun
865,000 mi
(1,392,000 km)

Jupiter
89,000 mi
(143,000 km)

Saturn
74,900 mi
(120,600 km)

Neptune
31,000 mi
(50,000 km)

Venus
7,500 mi
(12,100 km)

Mars
4,200 mi
(6,800 km)

Mercury
3,000 mi
(4,900 km)

Earth
7,940 mi
(12,780 km)

Uranus
32,000 mi
(51,000 km)

Sizes given are the approximate diameter of each body.

A comet is a small chunk of dust and ice that orbits the sun. Comet West, seen here, was named after the astronomer who discovered it, Richard West.

objects called the Milky Way **galaxy**. Just as the planets in the solar system revolve around the sun, the stars in the Milky Way revolve around its nucleus, or center. It takes the sun about 200 million years to travel around the nucleus of the Milky Way.

The Pinwheel Galaxy, seen here, has the same spiral shape as the Milky Way. The galaxy is also known as M33. It is one of the closest galaxies to our own.

Viewed from above, the Milky Way looks like a giant pinwheel. The stars are gathered in the flat shape of a disk, and arms of stars spiral out from the nucleus.

The Milky Way is just one of billions of galaxies in the universe. They probably formed billions of years ago, soon after the universe began. Most galaxies move through the universe as part of clusters, or groups, of galaxies. The Milky Way is at

On a dark, clear night, a dusty white band of stars can be seen stretching across the sky. It is a massive collection of stars, dust, and clouds of gas called the Milky Way galaxy.

one end of a cluster called the Local Group. It includes about forty galaxies. The largest galaxy in the Local Group is the Andromeda Galaxy.

Even the smaller galaxies are made up of millions of stars. The Milky Way is about twenty times larger than a smaller galaxy. It contains hundreds of billions of stars. The largest galaxies contain trillions of stars.

COMPARE AND CONTRAST

How is a galaxy similar to the solar system? How is it different?

On the Job

Astronomers study many different parts of the universe. Some astronomers concentrate on the planets or on how galaxies are formed. Others focus on the sun or other stars, learning how they change over time.

Observational astronomers use tools to record data from space. They then use that data to test an idea about space. Other astronomers use computers to make models of space objects to understand how they work.

To become an astronomer, you must take many courses in math and science. You

Modern astronomers rely on advanced technology to do their work. This astronomer is using a telescope at the Royal Observatory in Greenwich, England.

Incredible photographs that professional astronomers have taken and study are available to everyone online.

also have to be able to explain your discoveries to other people in written articles. Most astronomers may study nine or more years at a university to earn a doctoral degree in astronomy or physics. After astronomers earn their degrees, they can teach, work at government agencies, or work for private companies.

THINK ABOUT IT
Why do you think a person has to study for so many years to become an astronomer?

From the Lab to Space

Some astronomers get to travel into space as astronauts, but most do their work from Earth. They may work in observatories. An observatory is a place for observing, or studying, natural objects and events. Observatories have special instruments for gathering information about stars, planets, comets, and other things outside Earth's atmosphere.

Astronomers also work in laboratories. There they study samples of objects that have been collected by astronauts and

This is Palomar Observatory, located on Mount Palomar in southern California. Observatories are often located far away from city lights, to give astronomers a clear view of the night sky.

spacecraft. These include meteorites, rock samples from the moon, and dust particles.

Many astronomers work at colleges, where they teach and do research. Many others work for museums or for government agencies, such as the National Aeronautics and Space Administration (NASA). A smaller amount of astronomers work for businesses, using their knowledge of instruments and space to make products more advanced.

These NASA scientists are working on lenses for a camera that will record images of space.

COMPARE AND CONTRAST

How are an observatory and a laboratory alike? How are they different?

Signals from Space

Most scientists can actually touch the objects they are studying. A botanist, for example, gets to examine plants and perform experiments on them. Most astronomers are not so lucky. Only a small number of astronomers get to work with actual objects from space, such as meteorites or rocks collected from the moon. The other objects that astronomers study are much too far away to observe directly.

How, then, do astronomers find out about objects in space? Most of their information comes from electromagnetic radiation. This is

61016,7

Meteorites are pieces of rock or metal that have fallen to the ground from outer space. They are often stored in protective cases and handled with care.

Many more stars exist than the ones seen through telescopes. Astronomers can detect the presence of unseen stars with instruments that read the electromagnetic energy that the stars give off.

energy that objects in space give off. The light that comes from the sun is electromagnetic energy. Sunlight is a visible form of radiation. Other forms are not visible to us. However, astronomers can use special instruments to observe and record all of the different forms of radiation.

THINK ABOUT IT

Why would astronomers need information other than visible forms of light to be able to study objects in space?

Getting the Message

M any astronomers observe distant objects with the help of telescopes. Telescopes range in size. Some are small enough to be carried by hand. Large telescopes are often housed in observatories.

Optical telescopes use lenses or mirrors to allow a person to see an object that is far away. The lenses bend visible light and focus an image onto an eyepiece. Mirrors can reflect a stronger image to the eyepiece. Some telescopes use both lenses and mirrors for the clearest view. Early

Optical telescopes are also known as light telescopes. Light telescopes that use just lenses are refracting telescopes. Ones that also use mirrors are reflecting telescopes.

has been orbiting Earth since April 1990. It allows astronomers to get a better view of objects in outer space than they could get from Earth. The telescope was named for Edwin Hubble, a famous American astronomer.

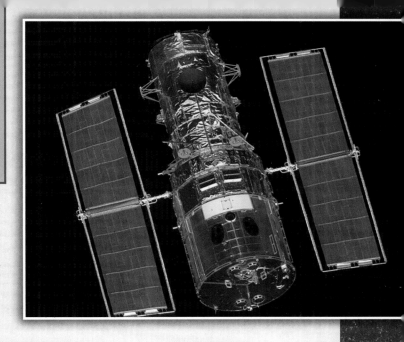

optical telescopes allowed astronomers to see the system of rings around planet Saturn and the many moons of planet Jupiter.

Optical telescopes can be used in space as well as on Earth. One, called the Hubble Space Telescope, is in orbit around Earth as a floating observatory. The Hubble magnifies and records images of distant space objects. It then sends the information to astronomers on Earth.

COMPARE AND CONTRAST

How is the Hubble Space Telescope like hand-held telescopes? How is it different?

Some types of telescopes do not collect visible light. These telescopes collect other forms of radiation from space—for example, radio waves, infrared radiation, and X-rays. Planets, stars, gas, and other things in space give off these types of energy. Radio telescopes look like huge bowls. They collect radio waves that travel to Earth's surface. Some types of radiation cannot reach Earth's surface. In order to capture that radiation astronomers use special types of telescopes that are mounted on spacecraft.

All these telescopes let scientists gather information about things in space that cannot necessarily be seen. For example,

This group of radio telescopes has been placed in a wide, open area, so that the telescopes can receive signals easily.

The Hubble Space Telescope produces images that astronomers could not get from a telescope on Earth. It is the source of this photo of the Butterfly Nebula. A nebula is a cloud of gas and dust. Some nebulas glow when they reflect light from or are heated by nearby stars.

they have shown that there is water vapor in other parts of the Milky Way galaxy. They have also helped scientists understand how stars and planets form and how stars die.

Astronomers also use cameras and other instruments to record information about distant objects. Photographs provide astronomers with a visual record of their observations.

THINK ABOUT IT

Why are radio telescopes important tools for astronomers?

Colorful Data

Photographs taken by high-powered telescopes help us take a closer look at stars. Stars appear to have different colors. The different colored light that they give off is related to their different temperatures.

The electromagnetic radiation that stars and other space objects send out moves through space in waves. The different types of radiation have different measurements called wavelengths and frequencies. A special instrument can separate radiation into the different wavelengths and frequencies. For example, the instrument shows just how much light of each wavelength a star gives off. Each wavelength of visible light is a different color. The range of

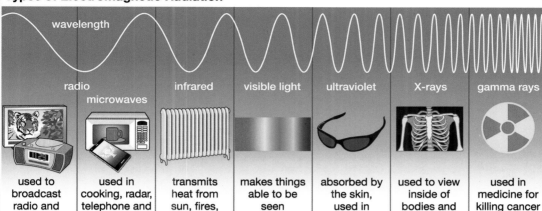

Types of Electromagnetic Radiation

wavelength

radio / microwaves	infrared	visible light	ultraviolet	X-rays	gamma rays
used to broadcast radio and television / used in cooking, radar, telephone and other signals	transmits heat from sun, fires, radiators	makes things able to be seen	absorbed by the skin, used in fluorescent tubes	used to view inside of bodies and objects	used in medicine for killing cancer cells

© 2013 Encyclopædia Britannica, Inc.

wavelengths makes up the **spectrum** of the star.

The color of a star is an indication of its temperature. Red light has less energy than blue light. A reddish star must have a large amount of its energy in red light. A white or bluish star has a larger amount of higher-energy blue light, so it must be hotter than the reddish star.

The electromaganetic spectrum includes various types of electromagnetic radiation. Radio waves have the longest wavelength and gamma rays have the shortest wavelength.

VOCABULARY

A **spectrum** is a full range or series of things, such as the seven colors that together make up visible light.

A Model Sky

Since astronomers have few chances to physically examine objects in space, they use computer technology to help them in their work. Astronomers create models on computers. The models represent how space matter has behaved in the past and how it might behave in the future.

These computer programs rely on the laws of physics, a field of science that studies how matter and energy interact.

Today's astronomers rely on computers to organize and interpret the data they gather.

Computer models can predict the behavior of these stars in years to come. They have already helped astronomers learn a lot about how stars and galaxies form.

Using these laws, astronomers can make educated guesses about what happens in space. They are never perfect, because so much about space is unknown, but they get better as astronomers learn more.

Computer modeling by astronomers has shown us how stars, planet systems, galaxies, and even the universe change over time. Computer modeling has become more important over time, as the technology has improved.

THINK ABOUT IT

Why is computer modeling so important in astronomy?

Astronomy All-Stars

The most influential ancient astronomer was Ptolemy of Alexandria, Egypt. In the second century BCE, he said that Earth was the center of the universe. He thought that the other objects revolved around Earth. Most people believed this idea of Ptolemy's for more than a thousand years.

In 1543 Polish astronomer Nicolaus Copernicus published a new theory. He believed that Earth and the other planets revolve around the sun. People did not believe this for a while. However, in the 1600s Galileo Galilei, a great Italian

Ptolemy's theories about the universe dominated scientific thought until the Middle Ages. In his model of the solar system, the sun, moon, and planets revolved around Earth.

Copernicus's theory was that Earth and the other planets revolve around the sun. He is considered the founder of modern astronomy.

THINK ABOUT IT

Why do you think Ptolemy believed that Earth was the center of the universe?

scientist and astronomer, proved Copernicus's theory with his observations.

Later astronomers made discoveries that also supported Copernicus's idea. In the early 1600s Johannes Kepler explained how the planets travel around the sun in elliptical, or oval-shaped, orbits. Today astronomers know that Copernicus was correct, but there are still many questions about the universe. Astronomers continue to try to answer those questions.

Amateur Astronomers

It takes a lot of hard work and dedication to become a professional astronomer, but many people enjoy astronomy as a hobby. Amateur astronomers are people who are curious about space and make their own observations.

A person who wants to learn about space should start by simply observing the sky at night. Many people first learn to recognize the groups of stars called **constellations**. One event many people look forward to each year is the Perseid meteor

Amateur astronomers can spot many different things in the night sky—such as constellations, meteor showers, and some planets—with or without a telescope.

VOCABULARY

Constellations are groups of stars that form recognizable patterns in the night sky when viewed from Earth.

shower, which occurs mostly in August. You can see meteors—often called shooting stars—for several nights from most parts of the world.

Amateur astronomers who wish to learn more might think about buying a telescope. Handheld binoculars can also help you view a variety of space objects in the night sky. They are also easy to carry from one place to another.

Ursa Minor (Little Dipper)

Polaris (North Star)

Ursa Major (Big Dipper)

The constellation of Ursa Minor contains Polaris (the North Star) and the Little Dipper. Ursa Major, a constellation next to Ursa Minor, is home to the Big Dipper.

What's Next?

There is a limit to how far astronomers can explore using today's technology. New technology may allow them to reach a little farther into space.

Sometimes the light from brighter objects makes it difficult for a space telescope to capture anything but the bright light. A new device, called a starshade, works with space telescopes. Shaped like a sunflower, the starshade can position itself so that it blocks bright starlight before the light reaches the space telescope's mirrors. This lets astronomers discover new objects and learn about their characteristics.

The Hubble Space Telescope took this image of the Bubble Nebula. As constant improvements in technology are made, astronomers will receive even clearer images than this one.

The Bubble Nebula – NGC 7635 HUBBLESITE.org

This illustration shows how a starshade blocks starlight so that a telescope can get clearer images.

In the world of telescopes, bigger is better. The larger a telescope, the clearer the image. The largest telescopes used today have a lens or mirror diameter of 33 feet (10 meters). Several giant telescope projects are underway around the world. Scientists have plans to build a new telescope in Chile with a light-gathering surface of 80 feet (24.5 meters).

THINK ABOUT IT

Will astronomers ever be able to explore the entire universe?

Glossary

AMATEUR A person who does something for fun, instead of for pay.

ANALYZE To figure out how something works, or how the parts of something work together as a whole.

ASTEROID A small rocky body that travels around the sun.

ATMOSPHERE The layer of gases that surrounds a planet.

CHARACTERISTIC A special feature or trait.

CENTURY A period of one hundred years.

COMET A small chunk of dust and ice that travels around the sun.

DATA Information or facts that can be used in calculating, reasoning, or planning.

DWARF PLANET A large, round object similar to a planet but smaller.

FREQUENCY The number of energy waves, such as light waves, that pass a fixed point each second.

INSTRUMENT A tool or device.

INTERPRET To explain the meaning of something.

METEOR A chunk of rock that burns as it passes through Earth's atmosphere.

METEORITE A chunk of rock from space that has landed on Earth.

MODEL A copy or plan of something.

OBSERVE To watch closely.

ORBIT The path taken by one body traveling around another body, or to travel along such a path.

PHYSICS The study of matter and energy and how they interact.

PLANET A large, natural object that orbits, or travels around, a star.

REVOLVE To move around an object.

SOLAR SYSTEM A star and the bodies, such as planets, that travel around it.

STAR A huge, glowing ball of gases.

TELESCOPE An instrument that magnifies distant objects.

THEORY A general rule offered to explain events of the natural world.

UNIVERSE Everything that exists, including objects and energy, throughout time and space.

VISIBLE Able to be seen.

For More Information

DeCristofano, Carolyn. *National Geographic Kids Ultimate Space Atlas*. Washington, DC: National Geographic Children's Books, 2017.

Greve, Tom. *Astronomers*. Vero Beach, FL: Rourke Educational Media, 2015.

Lee, David. *A Day at Work with an Astronomer*. New York, NY: Power Kids Press, 2016.

Owen, Ruth. *Astronomers*. New York, NY: Power Kids Press, 2013.

Saucier, C.A.P. *Explore the Cosmos like Neil deGrasse Tyson: A Space Science Journey*. Amherst, NY: Prometheus Books, 2015.

Shea, Nicole. *Be an Astronomer.* New York, NY: Gareth Stevens Publishing, 2014.

Websites

Because of the changing nature of internet links, Rosen Publishing has developed an online list of websites related to the subject of this book. This site is updated regularly. Please use this link to access the list:

http://www.rosenlinks.com/SAW/astro

Index